Teach Your Dog
GOG
NORTH WALES
WELSH

Funny & surprisingly clever books. Love. Love.
DAWN FRENCH, ACTOR & COMEDIAN

Anne Cakebread not only has the best name in the Universe, she has also come up with a brilliantly fun book which will help humans and canines learn new languages. I am world-renowned for doing the best Welsh accent ever, so it's good to now also be able to speak some actual Welsh too. And more importantly, so can my dog.
RICHARD HERRING, COMEDIAN

Now he disobeys me in two languages.
LUCY GANNON, SCREENWRITER

The whole family love these books!
BETHAN ELFYN, DJ & PRESENTER

This looks like a really nice, fun way to start learning Welsh – great book!
DEREK BROCKWAY, WEATHERMAN

Teach Your Dog

GOG

NORTH WALES
WELSH

Anne Cakebread

y Lolfa

Thank you to:
Helen, Marcie, Lily and Nina, my family, friends and
neighbours in St Dogmaels for all their support and
encouragement, Carolyn and Marged at Y Lolfa for
Welsh translations and pronunciations, and
Aran and Catrin Lliar Jones of SaySomethingInWelsh
for their help.
Diolch.

In memory of Frieda, who started us on
the *Teach Your Dog* journey.

NB The Welsh in this book is what's used in north-west
Wales.

First impression 2022

Illustrations and design by Anne Cakebread

ISBN: 978-1-80099-182-8

Published and printed in Wales on paper from well-maintained forests by
Y Lolfa Cyf., Talybont, Ceredigion SY24 5HE
e-mail ylolfa@ylolfa.com
website www.ylolfa.com
tel 01970 832 304
www.ylolfa.com

I grew up only speaking English.
When I moved to west Wales, I adopted Frieda,
a rescue whippet, who would only obey
Welsh commands.
Slowly, whilst dealing with Frieda, I realised that I was
overcoming my nerves about speaking Welsh aloud,
and my Welsh was improving as a result
– this gave me the idea of creating a series of books
to help others learn.
You don't even have to go abroad to practise.
If you haven't got a dog, any pet or soft toy will do:
just have fun learning and speaking a new language.

– Anne Cakebread

"Hello"

"Helo"

pron:
"Hell-o"

'o'
as in 'got',
but
longer

"Come here"

"Tyd yma"

pron:

"T<u>ee</u>d umm<u>a</u>"

'ee' as in 'tr<u>ee</u>', with rounder lips

'a' as in 'm<u>a</u>n'

"Don't!"

"Paid!"

pron:
"Pie-d!"

"Goodbye"

"Hwyl"

pron:
"Who-eel"

'ee'
as in
'tree',
with
rounder
lips

"I love you"

"Dwi'n dy garu di"

pron:

"Dween duh ga<u>rree</u> dee"

roll the 'rr' a little

'ee' as in 'tr<u>ee</u>', with rounder lips

"Happy Birthday"

"Pen-blwydd Hapus"

pron:

"Pen-bloo-<u>eeth</u> Hap-iss"

'ee'
as in
'tr<u>ee</u>',
with
rounder
lips

'th'
as in
'<u>th</u>is'

"Congratulations!"

"Llongyfarchiadau!"

roll the 'rr' a little

pron:

"Ll-ong-guh-varrch-ee-add-a!"

put your tongue on your gums behind your teeth and blow

'a' as in 'man'

'ch' as in 'Loch Ness'

"Merry Christmas"

"Nadolig Llawen"

pron:

"Na-doll-ig Ll-ou-en"

put your tongue on your gums behind your teeth and blow

'ou' as in 'loud'

"Thank you"

"Diolch"

pron:
"Dee-ol_ch_"

'ch'
as in
'Lo_ch_
Ness'

10

"**deg**"

pron:

"**deh-g**"

9

"**naw**"

pron:
"**now**"

5

"pump"

pron:
"pimp"

6

"chwech"

pron:
"ch-where-ch"

'ch' as in 'Loch Ness'

3

"tri"

pron:
"tree"

4

"pedwar"

pron:
"ped-wah<u>rr</u>"

roll the 'rr' a little

"There's a queue for the loo"

"Mae ciw i'r toilet"

pron:

"My Q ee-rr toy-let"

roll the 'rr' a little

"Who did that?"

"Pwy wnaeth hynna?"

pron:

"Pooh-ee naath hinna?"

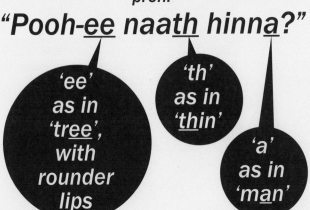

'ee' as in 'tree', with rounder lips

'th' as in 'thin'

'a' as in 'man'

"Be quiet!"

"**Bydd ddistaw!**"

pron:
"***B<u>ee</u>th this-t<u>ou</u>!***"

'ee'
as in
'tree',
with
rounder
lips

'th'
as in
'<u>th</u>is'

'ou'
as in
'l<u>ou</u>d'

"I won't be long"

"Fydda i ddim yn hir"

pron:

"Vuth-ah ee thim un hee-rr"

'th' as in 'this'

roll the 'rr' a little

'th' as in 'this'

"Have you got enough room?"

"Oes gen ti ddigon o le?"

pron:

"Oiss gen tee <u>th</u>igon o lai<u>r</u>?"

'th' as in '<u>th</u>is'

silent 'r'

"Who's snoring?"

"Pwy sy'n chwyrnu?"

pron:

"Pooh-ee seen chwrr-knee?"

'ch' as in 'Loch Ness'

roll the 'rr' a little

'ee' as in 'tree', with rounder lips

"Are you happy?"

"Wyt ti'n hapus?"

pron:

"Ooeet teen hap-iss?"

'ee'
as in
'tree',
with
rounder
lips

"It's raining"

"Mae'n bwrw glaw"

pron:

"Ma-<u>ee</u>n b<u>oo</u>-<u>rr</u><u>oo</u> gl-<u>ou</u>"

roll the 'rr' a little

'ee' as in 'tr<u>ee</u>', with rounder lips

'oo' as in 'b<u>oo</u>k'

'ou' as in '<u>lou</u>d'

"It's hot"

"Mae'n boeth"

pron:
"Ma-<u>ee</u>n boy-<u>th</u>"

'ee'
as in
'tr<u>ee</u>',
with
rounder
lips

'th'
as in
'<u>th</u>in'

"It's cold"

"Mae'n oer"

pron:
"Ma-_ee_n oy-_rr_"

'ee'
as in
'tr_ee_',
with
rounder
lips

roll
the 'rr'
a little

"It's warm"

"Mae'n gynnes"

pron:

"Ma-<u>ee</u>n gun-ass"

'ee'
as in
'<u>tree</u>',
with
rounder
lips

"Very clever"

"Clyfar iawn"

pron:
"Cluh-va__rr__ you__n__"

roll
the 'rr'
a little

'ou'
as in
'l__ou__d'

"Can I have
a cup of tea?"

"Ga i banad
o de?"

pron:

"Gah ee
ban-add o deh?"

'o'
as in
'g<u>o</u>t'

“Can I have the ball?”

“Ga i’r bêl?”

pron:

“Gah ee-rr behl?”

roll the ‘rr’ a little

"Lie down!"

"Gorwedd lawr!"

pron:

"Gorr-wath lou-rr!"

roll the 'rr' a little

'th' as in 'this'

'lou' as in 'loud'

roll the 'rr' a little

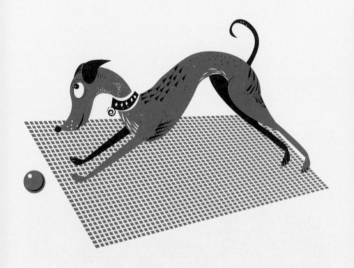

"Do you want to play?"

"Ti isio chwarae?"

pron:

"Tee-sho chwa-rra?"

'ch' as in 'Lo_ch_ Ness'

roll the 'rr' a little

'a' as in 'm_a_n'

"How are you?"

"Sut wyt ti?"

pron:

"Sit oo<u>ee</u>t tee?"

'ee'
as in
'tr<u>ee</u>',
with
rounder
lips

"Turn right"

"Tro i'r dde"

pron:

"Troh ee-rr their"

roll the 'rr' a little

silent 'r'

"Turn left"

"Tro
i'r chwith"

pron:

"Troh
ee-rr chweeth"

roll
the 'rr'
a little

'ch'
as in
'Loch
Ness'

'th'
as in
'thin'

"Go left"

"Dos i'r chwith"

pron:

"Dorse ee-_rr_ _ch_wee_th_"

roll the 'rr' a little

'ch' as in '_Loch_ Ness'

'th' as in '_thin_'

"Go right"

"Dos i'r dde"

pron:

"Dorse ee-rr their"

roll the 'rr' a little

silent 'r'

"Go straight ahead"

"Dos syth ymlaen"

pron:

"Dorse seeth umla-ee-n"

'th' as in 'thin'

'ee' as in 'tree', with rounder lips

"Go down"

"Lawr â chdi"

pron:

"Lou-rr ah ch-dee"

'ou' as in 'loud'

roll the 'rr' a little

'ch' as in 'Loch Ness'

"Up you go"

"Fyny â chdi"

pron:

"Vunnee ah ch-dee"

'ee'
as in
'tree',
with
rounder
lips

'ch'
as in
'Loch
Ness'

"Let's go…"

"Ffwr â ni…"

pron:

"F<u>oo</u><u>rr</u> ah knee…"

'oo' as in '<u>boo</u>t'

roll the 'rr' a little

"Don't scratch"

"Paid â chrafu"

pron:

"Pied ah <u>chrr</u>av-<u>ee</u>"

'ch' as in 'Lo<u>ch</u> Ness'

roll the 'rr' a little

'ee' as in 'tr<u>ee</u>', with rounder lips

"Goodnight"

"Nos da"

pron:
"N<u>o</u>ss dah"

'o'
as in 'g<u>o</u>t',
but
longer

"Good morning"

"Bore da"

pron:

"Bor<u>r</u>eh dah"

roll
the 'rr'
a little

"All gone"

"Wedi gorffen"

pron:

"Wed-ee gorr-fen"

slight pause

roll the 'rr' a little

"Are you full?"

"Wyt ti'n llawn?"

pron:

"Oo<u>ee</u>t teen <u>ll-ou</u>-n?"

'ee' as in 'tr<u>ee</u>', with rounder lips

put your tongue on your gums behind your teeth and blow

'ou' as in 'l<u>ou</u>d'

"Lunchtime"

"Amser cinio"

pron:

"Am-sa<u>rr</u> kin-y<u>o</u>"

roll
the 'rr'
a little

'o'
as in
'g<u>o</u>t'

"Bedtime"

"Amser gwely"

pron:
"Am-sa<u>rr</u> gwel-<u>ee</u>"

roll the 'rr' a little

'ee' as in 'tr<u>ee</u>', with rounder lips

"Bathtime"

"Amser bàth"

pron:
"Am-sa<u>rr</u> bath"

*roll
the 'rr'
a little*

"Stay!"

"Aros!"

pron:

"A-rross!"

'A' as in 'man'

roll the 'rr' a little

"No!"

"Na!"

pron:
"Nah!"

"Sit!"

"'Ista!"

pron:
"'East-_a_!"

'a'
as in
'm_a_n'

"Leave it!"

"Gad o!"

pron:
"Guard o!"

'o'
as in
'got'

"Fetch!"

"**Dos i nôl o!**"

pron:

"Dorse ee norl o!"

'o'
as in
'got'

"Catch!"

"Dal o!"

pron:

"Dahl o!"

'o'
as in
'got'

"Do you want a cuddle?"

"Ti isio mwytha?"

pron:

"Tee-sho moo-ee-tha?"

'o' as in 'got'

'ee' as in 'tree', with rounder lips

'th' as in 'thin'

'a' as in 'man'